Kelly and Friends

Thomas Simmer

This book was printed in the United States of America.

Book Designer: u-ranz

To order additional copies of this book, contact:
Xlibris Corporation
1-888-795-4274
www.Xlibris.com
Orders@Xlibris.com

To Kelly

A cat for all seasons.

Acknowledgment

My wife, Irene, took most, if not all, of the photographs of Kelly, family and friends. Since space was limited in the book, other treasured photos of Kelly are nestled in a safe place. I think, in some instances, Kelly's soul was captured by Irene. Perhaps one had to have touched Kelly to appreciate this feeling.

My thanks to Mr. Mel Brooks for allowing me to make reference to and paraphrase that great line in his film, *History of the World: Part I*; "It's good to be the King".

The photograph of the duck on the lake, taken by Douglas R. Clifford, is used courtesy of The St. Petersburg Times.

Thomas Simmer

I

TRAMP

You've heard of Mel Brooks? The movie he made, "History of the World: Part I". Well to paraphrase a line in that movie, "It's GOOD to be the Cat" especially with the humans I have: My mommy Irene, my daddy Tom, my sister Valerie, and my brother Mike. They adopted me, Kelly, when I was about three months old. At the time, I was staying with a family named Kelly, who found me lost and alone and took me home, but they had a dog so didn't want to keep me. Thanks to the Big Cat in the Sky and a young lady named Trina, I landed on four feet with the Simmer family.

"Hi. I'm Kelly."

I could tell straight away there had been another cat living with the Simmers because I recognized the lingering scent. It wasn't until being with them for a few months that I heard the story of the other cat.

It seems they were at a Fourth of July picnic at Joan and Ted's house in Bensalem, Pennsylvania, a town northeast of Philadelphia. Joan is Irene's sister and Ted is their brother-in-law. Their three children, Lisa, Dawn and, "bingo, it's a boy" , Steve, rounded out the group. They would soon be joined by a visitor. Hey! There's Tom. Tom. He'll tell us about Tramp.

"Mike, me, and Valerie with Lisa, Steve and Dawn."

While Irene and Joan were busy preparing the food, Ted and I had been worn out playing the usual Fourth of July games with the children. The shade trees and lawn chairs seemed to be calling to us, "Ted! Tom! Come join us." So when the kids' attention was elsewhere, we slinked to the nearest lawn chairs to catch our breath, latch onto a cold Heineken, and contentedly watched our wives begin to bring out the picnic fare. Coleslaw, potato salad, baked beans, rolls, hot dogs, hamburgers—all appeared in their proper time and place. But, what really caught our eye and tantalized our nose was the specialty of the day; shrimp wrapped in bacon, which had been gently and lovingly grilled. We think it was this aroma that prompted Tramp to casually drop in on our picnic to mooch a meal. Or two. Or three.

During the meal preparation, Tramp made sure everyone got some attention by either smoothing our legs or allowing us to scratch his ears. By mealtime he had everyone sufficiently trained and it became a small matter for him to wheedle handouts from all. He not only dropped in for lunch, but also hung about all day and joined us for supper. He was only a kitten and his filthy coat didn't enhance his appearance, but with his aplomb and ingratiating manner he quickly made off with our hearts along with our food.

Later that evening—the mosquitoes having driven us indoors—we indulged in some pinochle and TV watching, while the kids, mosquitoes or not, were outside playing flashlight tag. We even found time to clean up most of the picnic leftovers. With all of these diversions and a full stomach, Tramp soon slipped from our minds.

But he must have sensed he had succeeded in his efforts to adopt us, for later that night as we were preparing to leave for home I discovered him strategically camped at my in-laws' front door. He was lying in that classic cat pose; body all tucked together, tail curled slightly under and along his body contour, front paws curled in under his chest, head tilted slightly down with his eyes squinted.

Thinking he had departed when the food left, his presence surprised me. I bent over and picked him up. Bad, bad mistake. He immediately began consummating the adoption with a deep rumbling purr. A purr that only the most ruthless of barbarians could have ignored. I called back through the screen door, "Hey! Everybody. Look who's still here." Another mistake.

"Oh! Look at the sweet thing!" and, "The poor thing probably has no place to go." were some of the comments made when the group saw Tramp in my arms, rumbling away with a purr that made his ribs heave.

Valerie and Mike squealed, "Let's take him home! Lets take him home!" Irene and I looked at each other, silently exchanging uncertainties and doubts.

"Doesn't he belong to someone?" Irene asked as she scanned the faces around her.

"No, no!" chorused Lisa, Dawn and Steve excitedly. "He's always hanging around here, and a lot of times we see him at different houses," Lisa encouraged.

"See, Daddy, see?" pleaded Valerie and Mike. "We can take him home. He doesn't belong to anyone."

"Well . . . . ? I don't know. What do you think, Honey?" I asked Irene.

One look at their faces told me all I needed to know. It had already been decided! This gregarious pussycat, with his fleas, dirt and all was going home with us!

*   *   *

Tramp was the first thing to be put into the car. I placed him on the front seat before going back to the house to gather our belongings. I left the car's front door open just enough to let the dome light stay on, forgetting that cats can see in the dark and he needed no help from a dome light. I hustled back to the house to collect our things so we could toss them into the car and be on our way. A touching sight greeted us as we said our good-byes and made our way to the car. There was Tramp sitting atop the back of the front seat busily cleaning his raised front paw, with the car's dome light spotlighting all of the feline majesty he could muster. It was as if he knew he was going someplace special and was making every attempt to be presentable when he arrived.

We lived in Delran, New Jersey. If we drove east on leaving Joan and Ted's house we could have been home in about ten minutes, but the Delaware River was in the way. So we had to drive north on US 13, turn right on Pennsylvania 413 to get to the Burlington-Bristol Bridge crossing the Delaware. We chattered about how Tramp would act when we got him home, how we would ever get him clean, where would he sleep—would he sleep?—and what to name him. The humming of the tires while crossing the metal bridge drowned out our talking. But heading south on US 130 toward home, our chattering continued unabated, full of enthusiasm and anticipation. Many names were suggested, but because of his tattered and shaggy appearance, none seemed more fitting than—Tramp!

When we arrived home, Tramp was given a generous saucer of milk along with some leftover tuna fish. Using a large aluminum baking pan with some topsoil from the bag in the garage thrown into it, we had ourselves an emergency litter box, which we hoped Tramp would use. We used a cardboard box padded with clean rags, which made a cozy bed. Tramp seemed to like it for he quickly settled into it and purred himself to sleep.

After a few days of cleaning on his part, with some help from flea powder and cat toiletries, Tramp showed his true colors; a satin black body with spots of pure white on one ear and nose, and four paws of pure white. A handsome Tramp indeed.

He soon became accustomed to his new home and surroundings and could be seen gallivanting around the neighborhood doing those things cats love to do; poking into and investigating every little crack and crevice, leaping into the air after a low flying fly or beetle, picking out a suitable snoozing spot to soak up his daily ration of sun. His trips always led him back home when he was tuckered out and ready for some serious sleeping.

One evening he did not return on schedule. Frantically we searched the neighborhood calling out for him. It was well after midnight when we gave up the search. We went to bed but a sickening panic made sleep fitful for all. Mike and Valerie took an extra long time to fall asleep, crying and sniffling over Tramp not being home.. In the morning we rushed to the doors expecting Tramp to be waiting to be let inside. We were crushed anew by his absence

The next few days were spent periodically searching for Tramp. We asked the neighbors in the hope that they had seen him. We ran ads in the lost pet column. Each effort brought fresh agony. Finally we openly admitted to each other that he was gone. Our only comfort came from knowing that for the short time Tramp had been with us he had been treated like a King. And in return he had given us love and pleasure. Not until later that year would a Queen magically appear to ease our pain and replace our loss.

II

KELLY
THE KING IS DEAD, LONG LIVE THE QUEEN

Our home in Delran was typical suburbia: a corner lot; a bi-level with three bedrooms, one and a half baths; a family room with fireplace; a scattering of trees and shrubs; and a BIG mortgage.

All the neighbors shared our sorrow when Tramp vanished, but our next door neighbors, the Schroeders, were the most sympathetic. They had a cute female schnauzer named Heidi whom they dearly loved and an independent black and white colored male cat, Gwenivere, who just barely tolerated anyone including the Schroeders. It was probably the thought of losing their pets, especially Heidi, that made them feel so compassionate toward us in our loss.

The Schroeders, Peter and Inge, also had two daughters, Emmy and Trina. Emmy was six years old and Trina was five when we moved into the house next to them. Having no children of our own at the time, we took special delight in having these two small charmers living next door to us. For the eleven years that we were neighbors we watched them grow into graceful young ladies. And even though they became somewhat sophisticated as they matured, neither one tried to conceal her unabashed soft-heartedness for animals. They were forever hugging and cooing over someone's pet hamster, rabbit, cat, dog—whatever was handy. And they loved their Heidi. Their favorite nicknames for Heidi were Liebchen and Schatzie. These were naturals since their parents were of German descent. It was not unusual to hear one of them saying to Heidi, "Komst du heir, meine Libchen" or "Ich liebe dich, mein Schatzie" whereupon Heidi would leap into her lap and snuggle into her like a baby.

Trina seemed to be more tender toward animals. What can you say about a young girl who notices a kitten has blood around its mouth due to a loose tooth, takes it to Irene to "please pull its tooth". Tina's concern for animals was the main reason we acquired Kelly.

So here is this saddened family with their pussycat gone not knowing what happened to him and here I am a few houses away, a lonely, homeless waif not knowing what's going to happen to me or where my next meal is coming from. Oh sure, the Kelly family took me in but there's this dog here and he is not very friendly; I think he doesn't like me horning in on his territory, so I spend most of my time keeping out of his way or hiding under the bed. Sometimes just to annoy him I snitch some of his food. I shouldn't do that 'cause he chases me and I wind up under the bed with him snarling and snapping at me. Good thing he's too big to get under the bed. And when I'm eating my food I always have to look over my shoulder waiting for this brute to show up and start hassling me. It's embarrassing. I have to wolf my food down like the dog does and not have a quiet, graceful, petite, pussycat meal. And then there's the stares and talk from the Kellys. I know those looks and that talk—they aren't going to keep me and are trying to find a way to dump me. I'm so sad and upset. Mostly I crawl into a corner somewhere and fear for my future, and have catmares about what's going to happen to me.

One afternoon I hear a different voice in the house, so I stir from my haven and sneak a look around the corner and see this young, cute girl talking to the Kellys. Oops! She has spotted me! Oh, no! I think she's the one that's taking me away. I try to scoot out of sight but she is too quick and scoops me up—and she is hugging and cuddling me and cooing in my ear? This is good! I snuggle in closer and she scratches my ears and whispers to me some more. Now she's saying goodbye to the Kellys and walking out the door with me. I don't know where we are going but I hope there won't be any mean-spirited dogs there.

With me still in her arms we walk across some back yards toward a house that has a picnic table and benches in its back yard. There's three other humans at the table: a woman, a young girl and a young boy. Suddenly all of them become excited and animated as my new friend places me on top of the picnic table. They are petting me, scratching my ears and swinging a twig in the air as I leap to snatch it.

Oh, oh, whose this coming toward us. I think I'm the only one who sees him. I hope he's not here to take me away. I'm having too much fun playing with these humans. Oooh! No tickling you two. Pow! Got you that time, but I didn't use my claws. Ah! Now that's better—a nice belly rub from the woman. Here come the kids again, snuggling into me. Bop! Can't catch me.

*   *   *

I worked at RCA in Moorestown while we lived in Delran. Upon returning home one late afternoon, I barely had the car in the driveway when the squealing and laughter of Irene, Valerie and Mike reached me from the direction of the back yard. I walked to the rear of the house wondering what was causing all the commotion. The scene that greeted me caused me to blurt out in surprise, "What's that?"

What I saw was my family being entertained by a spindle-legged, skinny, almond eyed kitten that was performing on top of our picnic table. The kitten had dark stripes intermingled on a predominantly gray tri-colored body and head. A tri-colored forehead and gray nose was the only interruption to the pure white of its face, chest and abdomen. Paws with a touch of white abbreviated its spindly legs. This kaleidoscope of color, along with it's green almond eyes left no doubt that it had a tabby and a Siamese lurking somewhere among its ancestors.

Six eyes where obviously enthralled by its antics since not a glance acknowledged my presence. Trying to gain some attention, I uttered an "ahem" and asked again, "What's that?"

Whoops. End of play time. The woman and kids have noticed the man and are talking to him. I think I'll settle down, rest and wash my face.

Irene said, "Hi honey, this is Kelly. You know the Kellys that live down the block don't you? Well Trina was at their house and they had a kitten there but they said they couldn't keep it because they already have a dog. Trina brought Kelly here hoping we could keep her. I told Trina all I could do was watch Kelly while she found a home for her. The kitten had no name so we picked Kelly because she came from the Kellys." Silence on my part. Reading my mind Irene quickly added, "Oh, we're not going to keep her." Meanwhile, Mike, Valerie and the feline "we weren't going to keep" continued to frolic on the table.

Hey! We're all going in the house. I think this is a very good sign. Maybe it's the miracle I've been saying cat prayers for.

Oh, sure, Mike, Valerie and Irene made some half-hearted tries at finding a home for Kelly. After several days of "watching" Kelly, we found ourselves cringing over the possibility of anyone actually accepting our offer. Within three days we surrendered; Kelly had already found a home.

Kelly's first evening with us was eventful only because Valerie, for some reason, didn't want Kelly in the house. We had just tucked Valerie into bed when we heard her crying. She managed to tell us through her sobs, "I don't want to keep her." Her turned out to be Kelly. We managed to calm her and she went to sleep but we never found a reason why she didn't want to keep Kelly. Through the years we laughingly reminded Valerie of this statement whenever Kelly was asleep in her lap. And Irene has not escaped a good natured sting when reminded of her "we're not going to keep her" statement.

Geez, I think they're going to keep me. I hope so. This is a nice house and the humans are great, even the man who is always lifting me and holding me in his arms while scratching my ears

The, 'I don't want to keep her', girl .

and talking to me. I have my own private toilet facility, personal water bowl and a special saucer where my humans put my food. I get snacks once in a while but I found I can get food from them while they're eating just by putting on my best pathetic look. I do wish they would give me more of a variety of food in my saucer. Maybe Morris likes eating the same food but I like mine to be different now and then—you know, salmon one day, chicken livers the next and maybe a mouse here and there. I guess I'll have to catch the mice myself

They gave me my own bed but I've been working them so I can sleep with them. I like their covers better. They're coming around to my way of thinking 'cause more and more I've jumped into bed with them and they haven't shushed me away. Even the one who didn't want to keep me lets me jump up in her lap to take a nap. It won't be long and I'll be sleeping in her bed too. Michael snores so I don't sleep with him much. I feel so lucky to

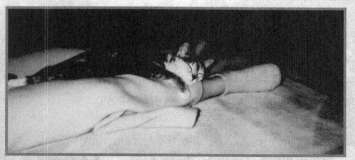

" Valerie's legs feel good, too."

12

be with these humans. They are so nice. Every time I see Trina I let her pick me up and I always give her kussas on the hand.

For the first few weeks we seldom let Kelly out of our sight. One disappearance is more than enough. At first her outings were restricted to our back yard with at least one of us carefully guarding her every move. Seldom was she left out by herself after dark. Gradually she became familiar with the neighborhood under our watchful eyes. It wasn't until we were fairly certain she was accustomed to her surroundings that we stopped tracking her, but we did continue peeking out a convenient window to check on her. Finally Kelly was allowed out in the evening. The first few nights we waited nervously for her return. Without fail she returned, ready to have a final slurp of milk to wash down the late night snack of dry food. Then, later, she favored one of us with her presence by curling up on the bed covers, leaning against our leg, happily purring and giving herself a final wash for the day.

We became less and less concerned about Kelly's whereabouts after several weeks as everyone got used to each other's habits, and it became routine for Kelly to come and go as she pleased. Her scrawny little body started to fill out with steady meals available and, judging by the way her tummy grew, the field mice in the vicinity should have been placed on the endangered species list.

III

Kelly Potpourri
Mouse in the House

Like most, if not all, domestic cats Kelly loved to bring her prizes home to parade them proudly in front of us. A number of times the mouse was still alive when Kelly arrived at our back door with the mouse in her mouth, and we were very careful not to let her into the house with her meal. Usually we could tell if the mouse was alive by the way Kelly meowed at the door. It must be difficult to meow with a live mouse in your mouth. There's usually a muffled "murk" or "merf" sounding noise. So whenever we heard a bonifide meow we would let her in and quickly take the mouse from her, wrap it in newspaper and toss it into the garbage.

But one evening she fooled us. The mouse at hand must have been sufficiently dazed to let Kelly put it down, give a normal meow, pick up the mouse and wait for us to open the door. Kelly walked smartly to the center of the kitchen and plopped her treasure on the kitchen floor. The mouse, suddenly revitalized, scooted across the floor and down the steps to the lower living level with Kelly, Irene and I, in that order, in full pursuit.

There goes my mouse! Don't tell me I have to catch it again. I thought it was done for when I dropped it. It was still, not even breathing — I thought. It must have been playing possum and gotten its second wind. Look out everybody! I'm on its tail again.

The mouse put up a valiant chase—darting under chairs, behind doors and among the logs near the fireplace. I finally caught up with it when it darted from the powder room and swatted it with a broom. We did the garbage can trick and vowed to inspect Kelly and her catches more closely in the future.

I know I saw that mouse come out of the powder room. I wonder if Tom swinging that stick had anything to do with it? I've looked everywhere for it and it's like it disappeared into thin air. Oh well, it's time for my bedtime snack and off to bed. Let's see? Who will I sleep with tonight? I'm still working on Valerie so I'll try my luck there tonight.

Heidi, Guenevere and Kelly

Kelly soon became the neighborhood cat because if there ever was a curious cat it was she. Her curiosity took her all over the place—a peek here, a visit there, now a snack from a friendly hand, nose and poke around every where. She was always welcomed by Trina and was always assured of some loving and a tidbit whenever Kelly visited with her.

Yeah, Trina was my favorite, after my family of course, since she was the one who connected me with my humans, And I always gave her licks on her hand to show my appreciation. I loved it when she scratched my ears and held me. But Trina had to do this when Heidi wasn't around, since Heidi and I—well, things were tense between us. Whenever we were in view of each other we would watch suspiciously waiting for the other to make a belligerent move. No violence ever broke out between us but there was a lot of watching.

Actually, Heidi seems to be a nice dog, not mean like the Kellys' dog. I don't know why we can't visit with each other. I certainly don't want to get into a scrap with her. But there seems to be some kind of misunderstanding, mistrust, hesitancy. I don't know how to overcome it. Guess we'll just stay with the way things are—she takes care of her business, I take care of mine. Now Gwenivere is something else.

The Schroeders had obtained Gwenivere when a kitten. I'm not sure how they came up with the name, but it must have been because they thought Gwenivere was a girl. It wasn't until Gwenivere had obtained some maturity, during a washing session with one hind leg straight up in the air, that Inge exclaimed to Peter, "Oh, my God, Peter! Gwenivere is a boy!" No matter, Gwenivere continued to be referred to as "she" and "her" by everyone who knew him, er, her. Gwenivere didn't play like a lady either.

You can say that again. I carry a few minor scars and have some bare spots where the fur flew from our skirmishes! We were always into sparring sessions—stalking, then springing and rolling about on the ground, kicking with hind legs and stabbing at each other with front paws, ears flattened back in threat mode. Now and then I would bite or claw too deeply and, Gwenivere, asserting his manhood—and his weight advantage—swiftly put me in my place with a well aimed swipe of his claws or a quick nip in a tender place. With some fur missing and a shrill cry of protest, I'd run for cover and in the safety of my own porch would tend to my sore spots and decided to wait till Gwenivere was in a better mood.

" Guinevere and me duking it out."

William Tell Overture

Then there was the parade. Sometimes when Kelly wanted to go out she would have to suffer the indignity of the parade. One of us would pick her up, cradle Kelly into our folded arms held at shoulder height, and with the rest of the family behind, each holding the shoulders of the person in front of them, we would start singing the William Tell Overture, while parading through the family room, into the kitchen, into the dining room, through the living room, through the hall, back into the kitchen and return to the family room door. All the while poor Kelly is jouncing up and down with tail curled over an arm patiently waiting for all this nonsense to end so she could go out. Finally we would let her escape but not before we showered her with hugs and kisses. She'd hustle out the door to escape these lunatics, stop and lick herself on the shoulders and wash her face and then toddle off to do her usual prowling and investigating.

The Parade

The Yew

We had a huge yew in our front yard by the sidewalk. It must have been eight feet across and eight feet high. This just happened to be a school bus stop for elementary school children. The cluster of children with their laughing and playing was too much for Kelly to resist.

There are those kids again out by that big bush on the corner. I think I'll just stroll across the lawn, mew now and then and wait till they spot me. I'm getting closer and closer—wow here they come! Can't catch me. I'll beat you to the bush. Whoops! Almost got me. Ahhh, I'm in the bush. I'll climb to the top where I can meow at them and they'll try to get me. That was a close one. I'll move to the other side. Oops. Too many kids over here. The other side looks like I can just peek through the needles and limbs.

The children played this game of hide and seek until the school bus arrived. Quickly boarding, they were whisked off. Kelly could be seen at the top of the yew looking around her as if to say, **"Hey**, where did everybody go? I'm not done playing yet".

The Vet

The veterinarian advised us to wait until Kelly was about six months old before having her spayed. When the time arrived we took her to the Vet's office and she had her operation. She looked so forlorn when we left her we almost cried. But it had to be done and because the vet kept her overnight for observation we didn't get to pick her up until the next day. It seemed like morning would never come.

Mommy! Daddy! Where are you? I'm stuck in this cage and my belly hurts. There's some kind of stiff stuff in my belly. When I lick it, it hurts my tongue. I hope I haven't been given away. My humans wouldn't do that to me would they? Someone's opening my cage door. Now they're looking at my belly. Now they're closing the door. I'm so lonely. I wish I was home napping on Valerie or Mike's lap. Even a parade would be good. I guess there's nothing else to do but sleep.

" Oh, my, yawn. Excuse me."

Yawn. That stiff stuff is still bothering me. I can't even give myself a good wash. What a girl has to put up with. I must have slept a long time because the sun is up. Here comes somebody. Yummy, at least I get breakfast. Mommy? Daddy? Are you ever going to come and get me?

Here comes someone else. They're taking me out of the cage and petting and cuddling and saying my name. We're headed out a door. Oh! There's Mommy and Tom. It feels so good to be in their arms again. I knew they wouldn't leave me. Lick, lick, lick, kussy, kussy, kussy. Let's go home. I don't like this place even if they gave me breakfast.

We missed her and the people in the Vet's waiting room smiled understandably as we smothered her with hugs and kisses when the assistant handed her to us. The other pets in the waiting room were too busy cringing and cowering under chairs or on laps in anticipation of their turn with the vet to notice or care that we had our Kelly in our possession once again.

The instructions from the vet were to feed Kelly light meals for a few days and to keep her from moving about too much. Especially no jumping or leaping. Ha! The light meals were a snap. The moving about was a world-class chore. For several days everything but absolute essentials was ignored as we spent our time keeping Kelly down.

I wonder why Mommy and Tom keep trying to make me lie down or stay on their lap? I FEEL GOOD! Especially since they took that stiff stuff out of my belly. Now I can lick and wash it without half tearing my tongue off. And it's great to be home and out of that cage. The people were nice enough, but that cage—brrrr. I wonder where Mommy and Tom are? I guess they've given up on keeping me quiet. Umppf. That was a nice jump but I missed that fly.

We were worn out. Kelly was frisking around as if nothing had happened. With the rationalization that Mother Nature—and Kelly—knew best when to move, we gave up and went to find some easy task to do like spading the garden or painting the house.

The Garage

Kelly hadn't been seen for a few hours one Saturday evening. "Well it's still early. She'll be along soon," we nervously told each other. But an hour after dark Kelly still hadn't come home and we were taunted by frightening thoughts and memories.

I've gotten myself into some tight spots before but was always able to work my way out of them. But this one is a doozy. I'm still trying to figure out how I got stuck in this place. I was just nosing around doing some pussycat investigation when all of a sudden the door comes flying down. I raced to it and tried to slip under it before it shut all the way, but no luck. Blam! It was closed! I must have been here a long time because my belly is growling. I could use a meal. Nothing to eat in here, not even a mouse. I've meowed myself hoarse, but nobody's found me yet. Gosh, I'm really hungry.

Valerie and Mike where in bed so we told them we were going to take a little walk down the block to get some evening air, this to keep them from getting upset over Kelly's absence. We started our search by walking along our driveway towards the street quietly calling for Kelly. Then we walked along the sidewalk, which took us in front of the Schroeder's home, still quietly calling out.

The sun's going down and it's dark. Nobody will ever find me in here much less see me. What was that? I think I hear somebody calling my name. It is! It is! It's Mommy and Tom. They are looking for me. I'm meowing my head off—I hope they hear me. This may be my last chance. Meow! Meow! Meow!

Suddenly Irene clutched my arm and whispered, "Listen! What's that?"

" I don't hear anything," I said softly.

"Listen! There it is again. It sounds like it's coming from the Schroeder's garage."

We moved toward the garage with me straining my ears to hear the same magical sound that Irene hears. She calls Kelly's name. And there it was—a hoarse and squeaky meow! We both dashed to the Schroeder's front door.

When the garage door was opened, Kelly came staggering out with the most pathetic mew I ever heard. Her curiosity had gotten her locked in the garage, and judging from her stagger and hoarseness she must have been in there for hours meowing her little heart out trying to get someone's—anyone's—attention.

The Schroeders were amused at the scene before them as two adults fussed over their cat with inane comments. "You naughty girl. Where have you been? We've been looking all over for you." Leaving the chuckling Schroeders behind us and shouting thanks to them, we hurried across the lawn to our house huddling Kelly to us and breathing a sigh of relief. After Valerie and Mike were told how and where Kelly was found, Kelly was given an extra special treat of raw hamburger with a large helping of milk. Her tummy was soon satisfied but it wasn't until the next morning that her voice returned to normal.

Big Mack

One of our favorite visiting spots, as well as Kelly's, was across the street at the Burns'. The Burns, David and Ann, were good company, a lot of fun to be around, and had much to attract Kelly: Two girls, J.R. for Janet Ruth, and Patty, ages 10 and 12 respectively; one boy, Billy, age 7 and all boy; ample lawn and bushes in which to romp and play; and an accommodating pooch named Penny who was very easy going with man or beast even to the point of sharing her food with Kelly all the while standing by with her tail swishing and that singular doggie smile on her face.

Most of the time Kelly would cross over to the Burns' by herself, regally, almost to the point of swaggering, she'd cross the street with head high and tail straight up with just the tip parallel to the ground to make what looked like a '7'. But, if we wandered over to the Burns' without her, she would follow after us, tail almost touching the ground, head lowered slightly, scurry across the street giving out with an accusing mew, looking for sympathy at having been left behind.

I just hate it when my family doesn't tell me we are going to the Burns'. They leave without me and I'm left to catch up to them. They know I like to lead the way in my regal fashion as the queen I am. But no, they take off and I have to stumble after them like some ordinary low-life alley cat. Oh yes, they know I'm upset by the way I meow accusingly at them with my head and tail down. And then they try to placate me by saying things such as, "Hurry up, sweetie. We're going to the Burns'." Hurry up indeed. Harrumph!

It was during one of these visits that the "Big Mac" episode began. A hot summer Friday evening found all of us in the Burns' kitchen. Kelly had led the way so she was content and busily sampling Penny's food as Penny lay nearby attentively, her tail lazily dusting the floor in approval of Kelly snatching her food. The adults were at the kitchen table sipping Old Granddad Manhattans. These were particularly refreshing on this hot evening since they came with a handful of cracked ice. They were the "drink of the day" when at the Burns'. Valerie, J.R. and Patty were lolling over their respective parents, now and then scooping a handful of potato chips or popcorn from bowls on the table. Mike and Billy were in the game room having their usual tussle of egos and periodically heated words came rumbling into the kitchen followed by stern admonishments from Dave and I. It wasn't uncommon that one or both of them sported bruises, scratches, and even shiners occasionally from their spats, but some mysterious bond kept them as buddies.

"One more of these", said Dave pointing to his Manhattan, "and I'll be ready for some Pizza".

Pizza? Pizza? Did I hear someone say pizza? I could go for some anchovies, sausage, pepperoni—any little scrap that I can garner from any of these humans here. I'll even share with Penny. Now she's my kind of dog.

"Oh, could we Daddy, could we," Patty and J.R. pleaded.

"Pizza? How could you two eat pizza after you gobbled up all the chips and popcorn?" I teased.

"We can always find room for pizza! Besides, you ate a lot of snacks too," countered Patty.

"J.R., did the Simmers see your turtle yet?" asked Ann.

"No, I was afraid Kelly might hurt him, but I'll go get him," she said as she darted from the kitchen.

"Where did she get a turtle?" asked Irene.

"I'll let her explain that," answered Ann.

" Here it is," J.R. said proudly showing a box turtle with a shell about the same diameter as a grapefruit.

"It's a big one. Where did you get it?" asked Irene.

"He was crawling in some tall grass back by our tomato plants—Daddy makes me weed back there—and I reached into this clump of grass and there he was," answered J.R.

"How do you know it's a he?" I asked.

"Daddy looked," giggled J.R., causing lots of snickers.

"Are you going to keep him?" asked Valerie as she touched the shell.

J.R. said, "Sure. I have a box with some grass in it that he can use as a home."

"He probably won't last long in there," I said. "Have you given him a name yet?"

" I named him Big Mac. Why do you say he won't last long ?"

"Turtles are wild creatures. They like their water and grass and their food is strange. They eat insects, bugs—all sorts of weird things. You won't be able to feed him pizza. He'll be difficult to look after." I looked over in Dave's direction seeking concurrence as I said, "I think you should let him go." Dave nodded in agreement.

"But I want to keep him," protested J.R.

"Well, if you want to be cruel . . . . . . "

"Cruel? How is keeping him cruel?" asked a puzzled J.R.

"Cats and dogs are okay to keep because they're domesticated—used to being fed and kept by humans as pets. But animals like monkeys, skunks, turtles want to be in their natural surroundings. Turtles aren't used to cars, houses, canned food. It's just cruel to make them live all caged up".

"I don't care. I found him and I'm keeping him," declared J.R.

"Well I think you should let him go. Tell you what. If Big Mac isn't released by noon tomorrow I'm going to picket your house with a sign."

With that everyone guffawed and Patty and Valerie said." Let's go get the pizza! We're starving."

There's that word again. I hope I at least get some anchovies.

"I'll call Pasquale's and order. How many and what kind should we get?" asked Dave. Even Billy and Mike quit tussling long enough to put in their order. Penny and Kelly? They were their usual patient selves.

* * *

Noon arrived the next day. Using the side from a cardboard box, I made a picket sized sign that said:

J.R.UNFAIR
TO REPTILES
FREE BIG MAC

Fastening an old stick to it, I sneaked across to the Burns' front sidewalk. Kelly followed me over. She walked up and down the sidewalk with me a few times then, tiring of the game, sat on the lawn and watched me pace up and down with the sign. Her head looked like she was watching a slow motion tennis match. Penny ambled out, sat by Kelly and signaled her approval by whisking the lawn with her tail. Some woman almost ran over the curb as she gawked at me while driving by. Like Kelly, she too was puzzled by the picketing, but seemed to be more interested in the identity of the picketer. I managed to hide my face behind the sign as she weaved her way down the street.

Meanwhile Irene placed a call to J.R.. "J.R., what's going on in front of your house?"

J.R. appeared with the rest of her family and when I spotted her I shouted a few times, "Free Big Mac! Free Big Mac!" J.R. rushed over to me and started to tickle me saying, "Oh, you, Mr. Simmer."

Both families had a good laugh over these shenanigans. J.R. freed Big Mac that weekend because " I didn't want him to suffer being caged."

Big Mac was crushed to death the same day by the wheels of a car driven by an unseeing or uncaring driver. J.R. handled the sight of her crushed Big Mac with some tears. I was devastated. If only I hadn't suggested she let Big Mac go! It was supposed to be a joke and turned out to be a heartbreaker. Dave and Ann comforted me by saying no one blamed me for the accident.. But years later I still feel a twinge of sadness about how a prank brought Big Mac to a sudden and violent end..

The Flower Pot

Kelly instinctively knew how and when to use a litter box. We only had to point her to it. She inspected it, marked it as hers with the ritual brushing of whiskers and cheek against its side, stepped into it and, with a crisp meow as thanks, she christened it and then spent a few minutes tidying up and burying her deposit. When satisfied with her work, she stepped out and smoothed us around our ankles. Kelly seemed grateful for the box and we were grateful she knew how to use it without any training.

Kelly was meticulous about her grooming and appearance and very selective picking a site to bury her doodoo. A clean box was a priority and her cries of anguish coming from the direction of the box announced that, that chore needed to be done.

It was this fussiness that led Kelly to our planter. The planter was quite large—it contained a split leaf philodendron—and sat on a tripod shaped wrought iron base. It occupied a spot in our bi-level entry foyer, so anyone leaving or entering the home or going from one floor to the other had to pass it.

OK! That's it. A girl can only put up with so much and this box is a disgrace. I'm tired of yelling when it needs to be cleaned. I'm just not going to use it in this condition. Let's see? Where can I go? Not the toilet. I tried that once and almost fell in. It gave me a fright. You know cats and water. I could go on the floor in the small bathroom but that may harm something and then I would really be in a jam. Or I could go on the small rug by the fireplace or any of the rugs, but again it would get me scolded. Let me look around. I'll go upstairs and—wait a minute look at this big pot here on the landing. Why this is a perfect place, even dirt to cover my doodoo. I'll just, hup, jump into the pot and , ahhh, what a relief. Now let me just cover this up and I'll be on my way.

"There's that smell again," Irene mused as she passed the pot one day. "It's been coming and going for the last few days. I wonder what's causing it? I'll have to ask Tom and the kids if they know," she thought to herself.

The mystery was solved when Irene began to cultivate the soil around the philodendron. Humming to herself as is her wont, she loosened the soil in the planter but paused when she came upon an odd looking lump. "That's a strange looking piece of dirt," she thought. Taking a closer look it turned out not to be dirt at all but a clump of Kelly's doodoo.

"Why that little scamp! She's been doing potty in the pot dirt. At least she didn't do it on the rugs."

We solved the problem by keeping Kelly's litter box neat and tidy at all times.

" Guys! My box needs to be cleaned."

" Someone let me in."

Her Royal Highness

" I know the answer to that clue."

" Nothing but bad news."

" E.T. and me."

" I'm ready for the Easter bunny."

" This binky is pretty good."

IV

Go West Young Man

Life was gentle and good at our home in New Jersey. The kids were healthy and happy, Kelly was happy and so were we with family and friends close by. But the harsh vagaries of my occupation—military electronics—soon caught up with us. I was laid off from my job as an electronic engineer with little hope of being called back. We had recognized the possibility of my being let go, but it was still a shock when it happened. I found myself looking in through our front screen door earlier than usual one afternoon with Irene looking back at me.

"What happened," Irene said.

"I've been let go," I said.

"Didn't they give you any notice?"

"Oh sure. It's effective in two weeks."

"So it finally happened. What can I do?'

"Well I'll be getting several weeks of layoff pay plus we have some meager savings, so we don't have to panic—yet. I can only think of one thing to say. Until further notice, if we can't eat it, don't buy it."

Cincinnati

After about six months of sending out dozens of resumes and going through interminable interviews, I finally landed a job with a company near Cincinnati, Ohio. Irene was disconcerted by the news that we would be going to Cincinnati leaving family and friends behind.

"Cincinnati? Cincinnati? What's in Cincinnati," asked Irene.

" I guess the most important thing is there's a company out there that wants to pay me for working, and we can use the money."

" First you take the Pennsylvania Turnpike to New Stanton, then you ...."

This was in 1972, the time when the Big Red Machine was just beginning to take over the world of baseball. Irene soon discovered and fell in love with Johnny Bench. Years later any hint of leaving Cincinnati brought cries of protest from Irene Not because of Mr. Bench, but because we had grown to love the area.

The company provided Irene and me with a three day all-expense-paid trip to the Queen City to look for housing. Irene's parents volunteered to take care of Valerie, Mike and Kelly while we were gone. Both of us were novices when it came to flying, so jetting into Cincinnati was a special and exciting trip for both of us. We picked up a rental car at the airport, and, armed with maps and housing guides, we scoured the area for a townhouse with three bedrooms and a bath and a half. It was our plan to rent for awhile and then leisurely look for permanent housing. We put two questions to each townhouse manager: Are children allowed? Are pets allowed? No to either one of these and the search continued.

Naturally we looked for a safe and comfortable place for Valerie and Mike, but I blushingly confess the townhouse we finally selected was because of a small field behind it which would give Kelly a safe place to romp. In fact, we wrung a pledge from the harried manager that she would hold a particular unit for us because its small back lawn was bordered by Kelly's field. To seal the deal we paid three months rent in advance.

There is nothing more tiresome than searching for new housing—unless it's searching for a new job—which our beds at the motel could attest to, having collapsed into them each evening during our stay. Exhausted from our search, we flew back to New Jersey warmed by a happy glow of success, secure in knowing we had found a comfortable, safe home for the family.

Zoom! Zoom! Zoom! My family seems to be in a BIG hurry for some reason. Naturally, I don't know why. No one tells me anything. Look out! You almost stepped on my tail, Mike. I think the best thing I can do is find a nice safe corner and keep out of the way.

There was constant activity as we prepared for the move; list the house with a realtor, arrange to stop the paper delivery, alert the post office of change of address, advise telephone and power companies when to turn off the service, set up the garage sale. There were skaty-eight things to do and no one had time to think, but we talked incessantly about how Kelly was going to get to Cincinnati She was petrified of automobiles. Every time she had to ride in one she became so upset she would toss her cookies. We had no clue how she would react to a plane and she certainly couldn't walk there. The plane would be the quickest way so we opted for that. And there would be no baggage compartment for her! She would ride in the passenger compartment with the family. The airline assured us she would be viewed as carry-on luggage provided she was in a carrier that could be placed on the floor under our seats. We did consult with our veterinarian and he gave some pills to give to her prior to the flight to help relax her.

We arrived in Cincinnati in two shifts. I drove the family car there one week before the rest of the family arrived since I had committed to start work before we could all make the move. This was in September and the leaves changing in the mountains along the western part of Pennsylvania's turnpike was spectacular. I took the turnpike into New Stanton where I spent the night at a motel. The next day I picked up I70 into Columbus, Ohio and then south toward Cincinnati on I71. About 25 miles north of Cincinnati I passed Paramount's King's Island, a Disney type theme park, and thought how Mike and Valerie would enjoy that.

My leaving early left Irene to deal with all the last minute details. The company paid for my going home for a weekend but even that didn't help to resolve many issues. The Schroeders and the Burns were always available to lend a helping hand. But, there was still Valerie and Mike to tend to, and Kelly's voyage also fell upon Irene's shoulders.

Don't tell me it's time for the Vet again. I hate getting into this carrier because it always means I'm going to get stuck with needles, be forced—fed some pills and have some glass thingy pushed up my heine and then this guy looks at it after pulling it out and says it's OK, What's OK? Why are we getting into this strange car? That's not our car. And this isn't the way to the Vet's. What's going on?

Wow! Look at all the people in here standing in lines and carrying or dragging box things with them. We're in line and Mommy is carrying me and now we're walking thru this long hallway with windows and what are those big metal things out there with windows and what looks like a tunnel connecting it to this hallway? Now we're going through one of those tunnels with Valerie and Mike in front of Mommy. Now we're walking down an aisle with seats and windows all around us and Mike then Valerie slide into some seats. Then Mommy sits down and puts me behind her legs and part way under her seat. I can just barely see out my carrier. I can see some people sitting across from where we are. Mommy lets me lick her fingers through the holes in my carrier—nice cool milk. I don't know what those pills were that Mommy forced me to swallow this morning—that's not my favorite thing to do—before we got into that strange car. I feel like I'm in a dream world. I'm so relaxed and calm and I didn't toss my cookies anywhere. Amazing with all that's been going on. I do feel drowsy so I'll just lay back and snooze and later on try to figure out what the heck is happening.

What was that bump and screech? Mommy is giving me some more milk so everything must be OK. I really slept good. I wonder how long? People are all jumping out of their seats and jostling each other in the aisles. All I can see are legs and feet. Are you sure everything is OK? Those legs and feet are starting to move and we all get in line too. Mike and Valerie are behind us and they both reach in and scratch my ears. Now we're walking and here we go again through the tunnel and now we're out in a big room with people milling around hugging and kissing—and there's Tom. Oh, Daddy are you a sight for pussycat eyes. You'll never know what I just went through. Tom hugs and kisses everybody, then it's my turn with some petting and talking and ear scratching. Here we go, on the move again and before I know it we're climbing into our car (How did that get here?). I'm let out of the carrier and it's good to stretch and snuggle up to everybody. We drive for awhile. Stopping. Tom gets out. Tom gets back in. Stopping again. This time we all get out, walking and for some reason I'm all wrapped up in a blanket. Can't see where we're going.

Somehow, someway Irene managed it all, and I met the group at the airport on a Friday evening. Mike and Valerie were thrilled by the trip and clamored for my attention to tell me about the nice cabin attendants, all the extra peanuts they gave to them—their pockets were bulging with the extra packs—and best of all how the captain had shown them the cockpit when the plane landed and given them honorary wings.

Kelly? She looked unruffled in her carrier. Irene reported that she had been such a good girl! "I had some milk with me and she licked it off my fingers through the holes in the carrier. We didn't hear a peep out of her the entire trip, not even in the car."

I guess so with all those tranquilizer pills in her.

We had reserved a motel room for the night since our movers weren't due at the townhouse until the next morning. Not sure how management would have reacted if it knew that a cat would be in the room with us, we didn't bother mentioning this when we checked into the motel. We trusted to stealth and Kelly's good behavior to see us through. Score one for naiveté, for later we would discover our surreptitious maneuverings had been unnecessary.

After checking in I drove the car to a parking spot near the room. Irene bundled Kelly in a blanket and with me in front of Irene, Valerie and Mike bringing up the rear—it reminded me of a prisoner being escorted by the police—we smartly and quietly went to our room and tumbled in. We gloated over our cleverness and hugged Kelly and told her what a good girl she was.

First order of business was to set up the litter box using a small pan and kitty litter brought along on the flight. Kelly used it immediately.

What a relief! I thought I was never going to see a doodoo box again. I did do a little tinkle in the carrier. I just couldn't hold it any longer. Wonder when we're going to eat? There's a knock on the door and hey, why are you shoving me under the blankets?

We had ordered room service, coffee for us, ice cream for Mike and Valerie and a glass of milk for Kelly. When the bellboy entered the room all he saw was Irene sitting in a chair and Valerie and Mike on the bed watching TV. He never suspected that a cat was quietly lying under the bed covers.

When the bellboy left, we threw back the bed covers and Kelly jumped from the bed with a curt **"brrit"** as if to say, **"Gee**, what a girl has to put up with. At least there's some milk and food to eat."

The next morning Irene and I took turns eating breakfast so one of us would be around to watch Kelly. Kelly got rewarded with some pieces of bacon and sausage for being such a good girl. Some ice had kept her milk through the night.

We repeated the blanket trick the next morning to get Kelly out of the room. Evidently a good night's rest made Kelly friskier in the morning and she protested this treatment with a few muffled meows and tried to push a paw out of the blanket.

Why are you doing this? First you shove me in a blanket to get me into a room, then you cover me up on the bed with blankets, now you're shoving me into a blanket again. There better be a big treat waiting for me when this is all over, if it ever ends. Let me out of here! Finally, loose in the car. Stopping. Tom gets out. Tom gets back in. Moving again and they're all laughing like crazy. Ha, ha, indeed.

We marveled at our good fortune that no one was around to discover our secret. As I was checking out, a stout, matronly lady approached carrying a Pekinese and I heard her comment to one of the desk clerks, "Lotus and I have decided to stay at your establishment one more evening and I wish to confirm our reservation for this evening."

I casually asked my desk clerk, " Do you, uh, allow pets in the rooms?

" Yes sir, We sure do. No boas, though," he chuckled.

" That's nice to know. I'll have to remember that the next time I stay here."

As we drove away from the hotel, I told Irene and the kids about the policy on pets and we laughed all the way to the townhouse about our unnecessary intrigue.

The Hunt

The townhouse served its purpose. It gave us a chance to catch our breathe and become familiar with the area. Valerie and Mike had a swimming pool and a playground to use during the season, a school they could walk to, lots of new friends and a friendly sweet shop nearby to get candy and pop. (In New Jersey pop would be soda, but in Cincinnati, soda is pop.) Irene and I had a new shopping mall we could go to and a new home that didn't require much maintenance, so we had oodles of time to explore the area. And Kelly, sweet Kelly, had her small field where she could hunt and poke and sniff around. As it turned out, it was only a few cat steps through the field and you were right in the middle of an automobile dealership. We often wondered how many buyers, sales people and mechanics Kelly met during her sojourns and how many she was able to con out of a treat.

After about six months we got serious about looking for a house. We wanted something that had at least 3 bedrooms, two baths, family room and a fairly large master bedroom and we always had Kelly and her needs in mind.

This turned out to be "search for the townhouse, part II". On weekends our bones ached, our brains were dulled, our senses overloaded from the search. Please, an end to this quest and just let us fling ourselves onto the comfort of our easy chair or sofa. Things became so tiring that at times Irene and the kids begged off and sent me alone into the fray. Just when we thought we would never find a home, we did, or rather I did, since it was on one of my "lone eagle" trips that the house we were looking for was discovered. I couldn't wait to get home to tell them about it.

What was that? Oh, it's Tom. I was really enjoying my nap on Irene's legs and then Tom has to barge in making a lot of noise waking me up. He's telling them something, waving his arms, pointing at them, clapping his hands together and they're just sitting and staring at him. What now? Tom sure is excited about something. "You won't believe the house I saw today! It's in a small town called Springdale which has a wonderful Rec Center and is in a great school district. It has four bedrooms, two and a half baths, family room with fireplace, basement, two car garage, big master suite, field in the back for Kelly, a-n-n-duh, are you ready for this? An in-ground swimming pool!"

Their stunned silence was punctuated by their jaws dropping.

What? Tom has stopped talking and waving his arms and their still just staring at him.
" I told the owners you would have to look at the house before we would make a decision."
More silence.

They're still staring. I look from one to the other searching for some clue about what's going on. Nothing.

I asked, " Aren't you going to say anything?"

Irene is saying something to Tom with a funny look on her face. Mike and Valerie are just sitting there with big grins on their face. They must like what Tom is saying.

Irene smirked and said, " You're making this up, aren't you? Getting even because we didn't go with you?"

Whatever Irene said has wiped the smile from the kids' faces.

"No, no. I swear. It's true. All we have to do is make an appointment for you to go through the house.. I'm sure you'll love it. Mike and Valerie, too. And Kelly will love her field. And I forgot to mention that it has a fence in the backyard, so we won't have to worry about Kelly going astray."

Whatever Tom has said made all of them happy. Irene jumped up so fast she dumped me off her lap. They're hugging and kissing and jumping up and down. I haven't seen them this happy since they found me in Schroeder's garage. Hmmm. Yawn. I think I'll resume my nap but with all this noise I may not be able to get back to sleep.

The house proved to be a big hit with everyone. We moved in in July, 1973 and while we were busy unloading and unpacking we put Kelly out into her nice, safe fenced yard where she couldn't get into any trouble and we wouldn't step on or trip over her.

I had to go through the cage treatment again and another car ride. And, yeah, I tossed them, but was finally let out of the car at an unfamiliar house. Good to get some fresh air. Now where's Tom taking me? Through the house, opens up a sliding door and plops me on some big, flat stones. This must be the backyard. Different than the one where I used to live. There's a flower bed wall. I'll have to check it out to see if it's a good place to soak up some sun while taking a nap. It'll also be a good doodoo spot in case I have an unacceptable litter box. Whoa, there's a swimming pool! I'll give that a wide path. You know how cats are with water. And there's a nice field for me to explore, but I'm fenced-in in here. I'll just nose around to see if I find anything interesting.

Later on when we were taking a break we walked out back to see how Kelly was doing. To our shock Kelly wasn't in the yard. Nowhere to be seen. While scouring the yard Irene spotted a hole in the fence by one of the corner posts and said, "Look. I'll bet she got out through here." We all called for her while looking down into the field and sure enough here comes the little scamp through the brush and weeds, through the hole and into the yard meowing all the way letting us know, "**Here** I am—did you think I got lost?"

There were plenty of friends for everyone. We had cordial neighbors all around us, and the neighbors had playmates for Mike, Valerie and Kelly. For Kelly there was Gabby next door, Mimi across the street and Jigs a few doors down the street. None of them mixed it up with Kelly the way Gwenivere did. They all seemed to be pals and were more than willing to cozy up to each other rather than fight over territory. Like us, the neighbors were heavily involved with school, soccer, little league and lunch money, but always seemed to have time for a chat or visit. We were fortunate to find this lovely place to live and live we did for over thirty years.

" My new house showing my corner. Plays a big part in in this story."

V

More Potpourri
Almost an Angel

Kelly is well behaved, but she's no angel. She does certain no-no's and naughties now and then that she knows very well she isn't supposed to be doing; leaping atop the kitchen counter investigating for possible leftovers, rooting around in the waste can, perhaps attracted by discarded chicken bones, digging in our garden and using it as a litter box, scratching unworthy food from her dish onto the floor and then showing her complete distain, try to bury it by pawing the floor, opening kitchen and bathroom cabinet doors located near the floor and then scattering the contents or maybe nibble away at a roll of bathroom tissue. We have barked our shins on many a cabinet door thought to be closed. Most of her transgressions are minor annoyances and being as spoiled as she is she usually gets away with a few sharp words or warnings directed at her. Her reaction to these is to hunker down and creep away. Sometimes we use the old rolled-up-newspaper trick and smack it against our leg in admonishment accompanied with "you naughty girl".

Her reaction to this is to flee the area for some comforting place such as the pillows on Valerie's bed.

Escaped again! They think I run away from that paper 'cause I'm scared to be scolded. I'm wise to that trick. I run just to make them think they've scolded me again, but I really run so I can hide under the bed and take a nap. By the time I wake up I know they're sorry and ready to greet me like the Princess I am. Guess I'll just saunter on down stairs and be greeted by their apology. I really love those guys, but they are soooo easy.

After we have been amply

"Just washing up before my nap."

" Nap time!"

chastised by her prolonged absence, she reappears to be greeted with, "There you are my sweetie, did you have a nice nap?" Or, "Where was you my love, we was looking for you? Do you want to go out now?"

Assured by our soothing babble that she still has us trained and that we are completely contrite, Kelly stretches lazily and unhurried, accepts our offer with a mellow meow and saunters toward the door. As we let her out, we complete the atonement with more babble, "Of course my babushka, but first come and give us hugs and kussas." All is forgiven in a shower of prattle.

KELLY JUST WANTS TO BE WITH US

Kelly has all the quirks and traits of a cat: The sudden mad dash through the house for no apparent reason; skulking behind the curtain and swiping at a passing leg or ball tossed her way; acting as finicky as Morris; poking into, climbing on, snooping about; leaping under the Christmas tree and jabbing at the balls; being present when gifts are opened so she can investigate and approve each package as it is opened and then for a finale, charging into the pile of ribbons and wrapping paper and scattering them under tables and chairs. One trait of Kelly's that few, if any other, cats have is her willingness to lick us on hand, arm or face when asked to "give us a Kussa".

Hey, Tom's got his legs stretched out on the stool in front of his chair. I love to sleep on his legs, they are so warm and it's really great when he has a blanket over them. Now that's really snuggle time. I'll just leap up there and settle in. Here comes the hand so I guess I'll have to give him some kussas. Lick, lick, lick. There. He seems to be satisfied. Now for some big time napping.

But the trait that made Kelly particularly dear to us is her penchant to be with any or all of us. If we're relaxing

" Tom always gets grouchy at tax time, but his legs are always good for a nap."

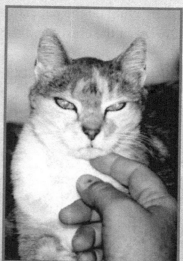

" I don't know? Should I give him a kussa?"

35

Going.   Going.   Gone!

on the porch, Kelly will be there mewing and smoothing to remind us of her presence. Then she'll stroll to the end of the porch, look around the corner of the house, view the surroundings for a few moments, then repeat the mewing and smoothing. As she so often did at the Burns' she'll tag along when we are visiting neighbors. If we are outside she'll be socializing with the gathering, or if we had gone inside the neighbor's house she'd wait patiently until we reappeared.

"Being with" meant having a ball of fur jump into your lap and start licking the arm you are writing with; help you collect stamps; help make the bed but really only wanted an excuse to curl under the covers while purring away; help plan a trip by languishing on the map; help with homework by lying on the papers while busily investigating the pencil, now and then lifting a paw to playfully tap at the eraser end as you attempt to write. On one such occasion, I was doing some

paperwork at the kitchen table. One of my pink pearl erasers was near the edge of the table when a paw appeared and made a stab at the eraser, then another stab and then the eraser disappeared over the edge in the grasp of the paw.

Kelly was so involved in a garage sale with her snooping and poking around on the tables, investigating each visitor, and tagging after us, we finally hung a sign on her neck saying, "NOT FOR SALE".

Tom! Tom! Wait for me. You know how much I like walking down into the park with you. Wait. Wait. I have to sharpen my claws. He didn't stop. Now I'll have to run to catch up to him. He's gonna get a brrrt from me to show my displeasure. Maybe not. It's too much fun walking with him and I don't want to hurt his feelings.

Once in a while I would go down our terraced back yard into the park area behind our home. The city had turned Kelly's field into a Little League field with swings and slides in a separate area. Kelly would invariably tail along behind me and always make a stop at an old log to sharpen her claws, and then scurry along to catch up to me. If I stopped to watch the ballplayers, Kelly would stop and watch too. When I got to the top of the hill leading down to the swings and slides, I would usually sit down to enjoy whatever activity was going on. And so would Kelly. She'd squat down next to me and stare in the same direction as I, enjoying the baseball or soccer game right along with me.

The Pocket Park

" Tom and me in the Pocket Park."

" Tom and me watching the ball game."

" My scratching log."

THE NOSE

The kids and I took turns vacuuming and cleaning the pool. It was relatively easy and only took about a half an hour thanks to the vinyl liner, the vacuum and a cleaning brush with a telescoping handle on it.

It was my turn so I went over to the skimmer area to take the cover off so I could clean out the basket which kept leaves, grass clippings and other debris from entering the filter. Sometimes I found things floating around in the skimmer, all of which I would rather not have seen. Squirrels, moles, rabbits, and mice were some of the creatures who had met their fate in our pool. I soon learned to slide the cover off little by little so the shock of seeing a floating carcass in the skimmer basket didn't hit me all at once. When a victim was found, I'd grab the wire handle on the basket and with some deft maneuvering was able most of the time to bring the poor creature out without touching it. Then the ritual burying would be performed; wrap the body in newspaper and chuck the bundle into the garbage can. We never were able to tell if these were things chased into the pool by Kelly or whether they had fallen in when leaning over the edge of the pool to get a drink. On this particular day, I was in the process of sliding the skimmer cover and when it was about half way off I spotted a mouse with both small front feet clutching for dear life onto the basket's wire handle, the little black nose just barely above the water and eyes that seemed to be imploring, "Please! Please! Get me out of here!"

I did my trick with the basket and laid it on it's side so the little critter could escape. It staggered out of the basket looking like a drowned mouse, crawled, stumbled and tumbled across the cement walk, coughing and gasping all the way and disappeared into the tall grass of the lawn. Only the rustling of the grass revealed it's presence and progress, and the last I saw of it was when it dragged itself under the chain link fence surrounding the pool, probably to become a meal for an enterprising predator. It was one victim our pool did not get to claim.

SPRINGTIME VISITORS

There were two visitors to our pool who looked upon it as a haven rather than a death trap. Of course they were never around when the pool was opened for the season. They always showed up in the spring while the pool was still covered. The cover always collected a substantial amount of water from rain and snow during the fall and winter months so that it became a small lake about a foot deep complete with leaves, grass, worms, water bugs, small frogs and other denizens of the deep, some of which sunk to the bottom while others frolicked or floated in the "lake".

Our two visitors were ducks. One a green headed mallard with his squeeze, a mottled brown female. They both would come flying toward the pool, go into their landing mode with flaps down, webbed feet angled forward and swoosh in for a splash landing. Both would then rise up slightly in the water, stretch and flap their wings, and then with wings settled back in place take a turn around the pool, now and then bobbing heads to the bottom with hind ends sticking up in the air, webbed feet kicking for balance, to select some morsel appetizing to them.

The Victor

Sometimes on their visits they would do that thing that birds and bees do. The female always looked as though the brute was drowning her as the consummation took place. When completed, "macho man" rose up in the water, held his head high, and with his wings stretched to the limit flapped them triumphantly. I always expected him to crow like a rooster.

In the meantime, the female having survived the mating was placidly preening herself and casually floating around in the pool. As if on cue, they both scuttled up the side of the pool cover, sometimes sliding back into the water and taking two or three tries before gaining the top edge, nestle themselves down on the warm cover, twisting their heads backwards to snuggle their beaks into their wings and nap.

As suddenly as they had arrived they would fly off, probably heading for a real lake nearby in Winton Woods, a Hamilton County park, where there were ducks aplenty. I sometimes thought our pool was their way of getting away from the crowd.

One day three males showed up at the pool. We assumed one of them was the mate and the other two were pretenders to the throne. Now that was a real free-for-all! That harried female looked as if she were fighting for her life with three testosterone loaded males jumping and squabbling for position. Several times we thought the female was a goner. As all three submerged her with their weight, we thought she would never resurface. But marital bliss won out as the two interlopers where beaten back and flew off to seek other conquests.

Kelly was always agitated when she saw the ducks. She'd sit looking out the patio doors making short, sharp, shrill noises that sounded something like "meet, meet, meet" with whiskers twitching and ears folding back and forth. One could almost hear her thinking, "*If* I could get out there you ducks wouldn't be in my pool for long."

For several years one of us would cry out in the spring, "The ducks are back", after seeing them splash down to begin what had become a ritual—the bobbing, the swimming, the napping.

One year only the male returned. He swam around a little, napped a little and soon took off. He came back several times, always alone, always hurrying off, and soon we saw him no more.

TAKE ME OUT TO THE BALL GAME

The ball field and playground that was behind our house was great for the kids in the neighborhood, and Kelly still had her place to pursue her cat activities. The park is called a Pocket Park since, except for three access walks it is completely surrounded by houses and the end of a cul-de-sac. This was also convenient for me during the few years I managed a Little League team because all our practice sessions and most of our games were played there.

Mike was on the team and Irene and Valerie were spectators as I both managed and coached at first base. Volunteers were hard to find. I had my hands full and little time to observe activity around me. Kelly would also make her appearance.

Now where did everyone go? My humans are forever leaving without calling for me to tag along. They know I like to go with them. There's a lot of noise in the park where Tom and I go for a walk. Let's see if they are down there. Yep! There's Tom standing near that thing that looks like a pillow. I've seen that before when only Tom and his team were down there, but it looks like another team is there also. They have different colored clothes on. And there's Mommy and Valerie sitting on some benches and Mike has that cage thing over his face with what looks like a blanket over his chest and he's behind one of the other team's guy who's got a big stick in his hand. I guess I'll go to that other pillow in the middle of the field where I always watch Tom's team.

The game would be progressing normally when suddenly the umpire would call, "Time out!". Engrossed in the game we seldom noticed that Kelly had decided to play right field, or that second base looked like the perfect place to rest. Our sheepish look was accompanied by chortles and chuckles from the spectators and players when one of us hurried to scoop her up in our arms, outwardly admonishing her but secretly loving her all the more.

There was a boy, Trevor, on the team who was very outgoing when compared to his teammates. Some of this was gained from his exposure to the Cincinnati Reds and, I'm sure, other major league baseball players through his father who was, at the time, a member of the front office for the Reds. Trevor was familiar with the batting stance of several well known major league players and it was his favorite method of entertaining the rest of the team and to show off just a bit. His other entertainment was running the bases backwards, hitting each base with his heel instead of his toes. He was very good at playing ball and except for his few peccadilloes he was like any other boy of his age.

Once or twice during the season I would receive a call from his mother who would inquire, "How would you like to go to the game?". Meaning the Reds game of course, silly. I would respond, "Who's legs do I have to break?" With a smile in her voice she would respond, "No one's, but you will have to take Trevor along."

"No prob-lem," said I.

And the drill was to drive to the ball park, park free, follow Trevor through the special gate for club VIP's where Trevor was greeted by the gate attendant with a "How you doin' Trevor", wave Trevor and his entourage through, and repair to our seats behind home plate in about the eighth row, cha, cha, cha. Irene could just about reach out and touch Johnny Bench. Things went swimmingly until one time when the drill veered off track. We got to the park where we were following a scampering Trevor but for some reason we were about ten paces behind. Perhaps he was anxious to study some batting stances. As he pushed through the gate ahead of us and continued his blazing rush to the seats, I thought, "Oh, no! We're going to be left out here with no way to get in!" In a panic I started to yell, "Trevor! Trevor! What about us?" Irene, Mike and Valerie joined in and we soon managed to get Trevor's attention over the din as a wary attendant held us back. With a blasé look, first at us then at the attendant, Trevor nonchalantly noted, "Oh yeah, they're with me." The attendant said, "Okay Trevor. Just wanted to make sure." Such chutzpah for a ten year old!

I managed the same group of boys in the Little League for three years. We played ten games a year and my overall record was 1 and 29! The win came due to a blessed rain-out when we, by some miracle, just happened to be ahead.

None of the boys complained about my managing skills, or lack thereof, and years later some of them, now young men, and parents in some cases, dropped by to say hello and told me that everyone wanted to be on Mr. Simmer's team because everyone got to play. We had unlimited substitutions, so if I had fifteen players on the team, I had a fifteen man batting order. And I would sub for fielders every inning. And besides, we had Kelly for a mascot. Several times it was one of the players on the team that carried Kelly off the field be it practice or a game.

The team always hustled in spite of our poor record and, with the continual losing, we had little to cheer about, but every year there always seemed to be a happening that made up for bad times. One year the second baseman and the shortstop turned the prettiest 6 to 4 to 3 (for the uninitiated that's shortstop to second base to first base) double play this side of Great American Ballpark (nee Cinergy Field, nee Riverfront Stadium). I always put Terry in right field since his fielding skills weren't all that good, and line drives or fly balls were an adventure and made me fear for his well being However, one year, staggering and circling around, he managed to catch a very high fly ball, his only catch for the three years, and the cheering from the team echoed around the Pocket Park.

Another young lad, Marty, lacked all skills for playing baseball except one; he could run like a jackrabbit. In fact, the others nicknamed him Road Runner. Another was named Bionic Arm—this was the time when the "Million Dollar Man" was popular on TV. But back to Marty. One inning he led off with a walk. The first time in three years he had been on base and I wasn't about to lose the opportunity for him to show off his speed. When he reached first base, I took him aside and told him, "On the first pitch, I want you to steal second and just keep going until you reach third." The opposing team was startled as Marty motored around second and sped into third. "Safe", cried the ump. We were losing just short of the mercy rule, but the catcher, apparently thinking we were trying to show him up when we were just having some fun, threw down to third on the next pitch, and watched helplessly as the ball sailed down the third base line as our man-of-the-year, Marty, trotted home to score. The greeting Marty received from the team made one wonder if we hadn't just won the Little League World Series.

After the game I told the manager and players on the other team that they played well and had whomped us good, and that stolen base thing was all in fun and not to make anyone look bad. The manager said. "Wow! That kid sure can motor."

And we may not have had any of these small triumphs if it hadn't been for the efforts of Arv Svenson the father of "THE double play" second baseman. Arv instantly became my hero, not only because he knew so much about the mechanics of baseball—how to slide, how to run the bases (Trevor not withstanding), how to hit, how to catch and he taught our young charges all of these fundamentals. And he had also been at Wilmington, a farm club of the Philadelphia Phillies, when the "Whiz Kids" were there just before they moved them to the major leagues. Granny Hammer, Del Ennis, Robin Roberts, Mike Goliat, "lefty" Curt Simmons, Richie Ashburn, Puddin' Head Jones, Andy Seminick! I lived and died with those guys as a young man, and here I was talking to and working with a person who had actually been close to them, talked to them, ate meals with them, hung out with them, maybe even touched them. WOW!! And I still feel the pain when I recall the four games to none World Series loss to the "Damn Yankees" in 1950. But they had Yogi Berra, Whitey Ford, Joe DiMaggio, Phil Rizzutto and "THE OLD PERFESSER" himself, Casey Stengal. All great baseball people, and along with Robin Roberts and Richie Ashburn, all members of the Hall of Fame. I still remember the scores: 1-0, 2-1, 3-2 and 5-2. We gave them a tussle but fell short by a hit here and an out there. Gene Mauch was right—baseball is a game of inches.

Jigs, Mimi and Gabby

Kelly's three friends kept her company for quite a while but things always change. First Gabby's family moved away. They were nice neighbors and we missed Gabby's constant meowing from whence her name was derived. Then Mimi's humans also moved but poor Mimi was left behind. Our first thought was it must be a mistake. We kept her fed for a day and a half and then her family came back and picked her up explaining that in the excitement of the move they all thought someone else had brought her along. A happy ending. Not so with Jigs.

Kelly was on the front porch with us and we noticed she was giving a lot of attention to a spot on her belly, constantly licking and slurping at it. Finally Irene picked her up, and ruffling through her fur, found a bare, raw area where Kelly had been cleaning.

I looked at the area and said, "I'm no expert but that looks like a bullet wound to me."

"Bullet wound?" said Irene. "Who in the world would shoot Kelly?"

"There are many people in this world who get their kicks from this sort of thing. I think we should take Kelly to the vet."

The vet operated to remove the bullet and said Kelly was very lucky for it had lodged between two vital organs. Half an inch either way and she would be dead. We gave Kelly extra attention trying to take care of her stitches and incision but once again nature and Kelly took care of them.

Mike said later on, "Whoever shot Kelly is probably the same one who shot and killed Jigs." We had our suspicions who the guilty party was in both shootings but had no proof.

Deja vu

I've gotten myself into some trouble before but I can't believe I've done this again—locked inside a garage with no way out. This garage door has windows so at least I can look out. I've been meowing for what seems like hours but no sign of anyone coming to rescue me. And I'm hungry and upset. Oh, I hear Tom calling me! Here I am Tom, all cooped up in here in the house next door. Now they are all calling me. I'm here, I'm here. I guess they didn't hear me because they've stopped calling me. Geez.

"Let's get Kelly inside", said Irene, "since we're going to leave soon and it will be dark before we get home. Has anybody seen her?" "I haven't" answered Valerie. "Me either" said Mike. "Not me. Come to think of it, I haven't seen her for quite a while. I'll go out and call her."

I went out and gave my standard, soft piercing whistle, then called, "Kel, Kel? Come on in," and then more whistling. She didn't appear so I walked around the house looking in her favorite resting spots and around neighbors' bushes, but no Kelly. When I told everyone that I hadn't found her, all four of us went out calling and whistling, but no Kelly.

Irene said, "We have to get going. The Lofton's are expecting us for dinner at six. Kelly will show up and be waiting for us on the porch when we get back."

Reluctantly we piled into the car and backed out of the driveway with everyone looking out the windows hoping to catch a glimpse of her. I made the usual left turn at the Gray's house and as we were passing by, a chance look at their house made me cry out, "There she is!"

Irene and the kids jumped from the sudden outburst. "Where, Where?", they all shouted.

I backed up the car and pointed to the Gray's house. "There, in the Gray's garage. Can't you see

"Gabby and the gang. Amy, Gabby's human, is on Valerie's shoulder."

" This is my first lesson."

Gabby looking for a drink?

The building inspector.

" Just checking out the flower bed wall."

" Tom always makes a pile of leaves for me."

" Tom does nice work."

her through the garage door windows? She must be sitting on the roof of one of their cars to be able to look out of windows that high."

We got out of the car, went up to the garage doors, looked at Kelly through the windows and laughed in relief when she gave out with one of her "come save me" mews. So once again Kelly, the inquisitive one, had been snared by her nosiness and only by a stroke of luck had been recovered while she was still in one piece.

The Intruder

"Daddy! Daddy! I've been helping the skunk lady like minding her children and running the vacuum and cleaning and you should see all the money I've made", Valerie breathlessly reported to me one day.

"Skunk lady?" I asked. Thinking, and we have a hard time getting you to clean your room, I inquired, "Who and what is the skunk lady?"

"Oh, you know. She's Mrs. Short who lives around the corner and down a couple houses."

"Well, yeah, I know Mrs. Short, but why do you call her the skunk lady?"

"All the neighborhood kids call her that 'cause she has these three baby skunks living under her front porch. At night they come out and play in the front yard with the Shorts' kids and they even eat out of Mrs. Short's hand. They're cute!"

"You're kidding? Has she tried to get rid of them?"

"Sure, but everybody she talks to says the only way to get rid of them is to kill them and she doesn't want to do that. Besides, they're not hurting anybody."

"That's decent of her, but they're baby skunks. What about the mother skunk?"

" Oh, the mother skunk was there, but one day the Shorts' dog caught her in the basement and killed her."

"In the basement? What the heck was a skunk doing in their basement? I bet that smelled pretty."

"Mrs. Short said it took some time before they could get back into their cellar."

" By the way," I asked, "how much money have you made?"

"Let's see, I've been working over there , you know, off and on for about a week and she gave me FIVE DOLLARS," Valerie bragged, five fingers held up and apart for emphasis.

"That's good pay," I yawned and went back to my newspaper thinking how humane Mrs. Short was not to hurt the baby skunks.

* * *

While we were giving the yard an autumn spruce-up raking leaves, pulling weeds, and trimming bushes, we discovered a hole that was about eight inches in diameter and partially concealed under an evergreen tree and low-growing yews at the end of our front porch. Since it looked quite innocent, I remarked, " If it doesn't bother us, we won't bother it."—we soon forgot it and returned to the spruce up.

Not till late spring of the following year did the hole prove to be not so innocent for Kelly. Her habit of sitting at the end of the front porch, leaning against the side of the house and occasionally peeking around the corner to survey her domain, led directly to the chance encounter with the skunk which, unknown to us at the time, lived in the hole which we had stumbled upon last fall. We later reconstructed the crime.

* * *

It's nice out here this time of the evening. I can lean against the corner of my house, relax and keep an eye on the front and side yard. But it's kinda lonely since my three friends are no longer here. Purr. Nobody to bother me so I'll just take it easy for awhile before I go inside for the night.. Let's see—Who should I sleep with tonight.?

Irene and the kids were in the family room watching TV. Irene liked to sit on the sofa because it faced the patio doors where Kelly always showed up in the evening. With both paws on the door sill, Kelly would look through the door and give out with a meow, meaning I'm ready to come in.

"Has any one seen Kelly lately," asked Irene

"I did." offered Mike. "And she was leaning up against her corner outside."

"Ok. She'll be coming to the door soon," said Irene.

Hey?! Whose this climbing out of the bushes and onto the porch. Some black thing with a white stripe down it's back, and why is it lifting its tail and turning it's hind end toward —!! Ouch!

47

Oh! What a horrible smell. This stranger has squirted some foul stuff all over me; into my eyes, my nose, mouth! I can hardly breathe and it's making me gag. Mommy! Tom! Mike! Valerie! Come save me, gag, cough! My eyes sting so bad. I better run to the back door.

When Kelly appeared at the patio doors, she was frothing at the mouth, gasping for air, and pawing at her nose, mouth and eyes. Everyone panicked at this frightful specter. The kids began to cry and howl, "Kelly's gonna die! Kelly's gonna die!"

Thank goodness they can see me. Mommy! Mommy!

Irene leaped to the door and snatched Kelly into her arms, the foul odor now burning Irene's nostrils and making her stomach churn. Valerie and Mike began to gasp for breath and rub their teary eyes. Both kept up their crying and howling. Irene had her hands full and didn't have time to soothe them. Instead she barked orders to them.

Mommy has me now and is running toward the powder room and yelling and pointing at the kids. Now they're running off somewhere. Oh, oh, it stings and smells so bad. I can't stop gagging. Help me Mommy.

"Oh, no!" cried Irene. Some rotten kids have thrown gasoline on Kelly." The closeness and oiliness of the stench had fooled Irene and she didn't realize it was a skunk.

"Quick! Quick!. Kids, run and get some towels and bring them to the powder room!" Kelly all the while was struggling for breath and foaming at the mouth. As they ran for the towels, Valerie continued her wailing and renewed the cry of, " Kelly's gonna die!"

. . . .

While this was going on, I was returning home from a softball practice session where I had been helping Arv out. The car windows were down and I was enjoying the smells and sounds of a pleasant spring evening while fantasizing about leading my team to the Little League finals, when the shattering, unmistakable stink of a skunk broke my reverie. As I steered the car around the final corner to our house the stench became so strong I could feel the oiliness clinging to my body, hair, skin, clothes; it was as if I had been dipped into a cesspool. My eyes began to smart and my stomach turned a somersault or two as I gagged back my revulsion.

"Something got too close to one of the Skunk Lady's tenants," I thought as I pulled the car into the driveway not even suspecting that that something was Kelly. The engine had barely stopped when the kids burst through the front door of the house and sprinted the few steps to the car.

"Mom says for you to quick go to the drug store before they close and pick up a prescription for Kelly and she'll explain what happened when you get back," they gasped in unison.

"Okay," I replied as I started the car and wheeled out of the driveway. During the trip to the drugstore I just couldn't imagine what happened. It never entered my mind that the skunk odor had any thing to do with us. And the clerk looked at me funny and kinda' shied away from me. Guess she too got a whiff of the odor clinging to me. On returning home I entered the front door and started walking through the entrance hallway toward the powder room and with every step the evil, disgusting odor got stronger and stronger.

Hearing me, Irene called, "Honey, I'm in the powder room."

" Do you smell that skunk?" I asked.

"What skunk? I can't smell a thing with this gasoline on Kelly."

"Kelly has gas on her? How did that happen? Is that why Kelly has a prescription?"

" Let me tell you. Poor Kelly showed up at the back door all frothy and choking. I think it was some neighborhood kids who threw gas on . . . . . . "

"Gasoline?" I interrupted. "Are you sure it wasn't a skunk who got her?"

"A skunk? Why do you think it was a skunk?"

" Because of the odor. You can smell it all the way down the street, and BOY, when you get to our house it's enough to make you want to barf. Now that I'm here, I'm sure it's a skunk. I've never seen gas do that. What'd you get from the drugstore?"

"The Vet—I called him just after Kelly came home like this—prescribed it for her eyes. But he said to use this because I told him Kelly had gasoline on her. I wonder if it will hurt to use it if it was a skunk? Poor Kelly. Look at her. What should we do?" Irene said with a quivering lip.

Well whatever you do I hope you stop putting water on me. Not only do I not like water but I think it makes the stink worse..

I gazed at Kelly, who by this time looked like she had just gotten out of our swimming pool from all the wiping down with wet towels. Irene had been trying her best to relieve Kelly's discomfort—it didn't appear now that, "Kelly was gonna' die"—and at the same time be rid of the nauseating smell. Towels, rags, water, tomato

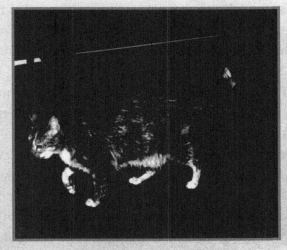

" Why me?"

49

juice, lemon juice, baby powder; nothing seemed to cut into that terrible malodor. Kelly seemed to be getting friskier too.

Hey! I've got enough trouble with this stinking stuff and now you're tossing all that other junk on me. I think I can do a better job than that goop, although the tomato juice doesn't taste bad. What a mess! I'll never get myself clean."

As I watched her, Kelly continued to clean herself even though Irene was toweling her down. Kelly would now and then test her right eye by carefully trying to lift the lid, but the presence of skunk secretion was still too strong. She'd quickly close the lid and resume cleaning.

"Kelly seems to be okay even though she looks ratty," I said. "I don't think the medicine will hurt her. It's probably some sort of eye wash so let's do this; put the drops in Kelly's eyes, through out all the towels and rags you've used, let's clean up the powder room and let Kelly take over the cleaning. I'm sure she'll do better than us now that you've gotten some of it off."

"Well . . . ,all right," agreed Irene. "We can keep watch over her to make sure she's okay during the rest of the evening. And take a good check of her before we go to bed."

For the next few days we closely watched Kelly for signs of after-affects. We kept a constant vigil on her right eye, which seemed to have taken the brunt of the attack. We remembered hearing about cases where people had lost their eyesight from being hit by skunk fluid. True or not we wanted none of that for our Kelly!

Happily, Kelly showed no ill effects over the next few days and she had weathered her discomfort like a trooper. The only thing that bothered us was when Kelly cleaned herself. Every time she did the moisture reactivated the skunk smell. For a few weeks thereafter we were able to tell where Kelly was without hearing or seeing her.

It was a few days after the attack during some discussion concerning the ill manners of the Skunk Lady's tenants; and that she should keep them on her own property; and that we weren't going to put up with our Kelly being attacked on her very own front porch; and that we would certainly do something about it if the Skunk Lady . . . . .WHOA! One of us remembered "The Hole". We had our own skunk! And this is what we think happened.

It was dusk when Kelly was in her position on the porch, the time when skunks, being nocturnal creatures, leave their burrows to perform those commands ordered by Mother Nature. Coming out of the hole and immediately turning and stepping onto the porch, the startled skunk found itself eyeball to eyeball with Kelly, separated by a distance of perhaps three feet. The yellowish-brown stains on the front wall of the house were silent testimony to what happened next. The skunk feeling threatened by this other creature, squirted an astonished and unsuspecting Kelly and scored a direct hit across the right side of Kelly's head and face. Both ears, the right eye, the right side of her nose and mouth were inundated by the foul discharge .

Any sympathy we might have had for any skunk disappeared with this realization. We determined to rid ourselves of that—that creature living under our porch, or else. After all, we protested, wasn't it a health hazard? Who knows what diseases and germs they carry or for that matter what they bring back to their burrow after their nightly foraging. And suppose Valerie or Mike or one of us happened upon it one dark night. We'd probably have to be put in isolation because of the smell. Why, we couldn't even call our house our own anymore for fear of bumping into that thing. We'd have to come inside at dusk every evening just to avoid running into it. We'd have to grow eyes in the back of our head. And its presence meant Irene and I wouldn't be able to enjoy those quiet evenings on the front porch when she sat in her chair and I in my rocker making plans or discussing the day's events. Front porch? Why we probably couldn't swim in our pool after dark for fear of coming nose to nose with it. And poor Kelly would have to come inside at dusk instead of being able to meander around her realm. Oh, you bet, that skunk had to go. And go it would!

But, wait? Just how do you get rid of a skunk? Their instincts for protecting their home are probably as strong as my brother-in-law's grip on a dollar bill.

*   *   *

My first phone call went to the city board of health. "Well, you see, sir," I said to the health commissioner, "we have this skunk living under our porch and we were wondering if you could . . . ."

"I'm sorry," interrupted the commissioner, "but this office doesn't deal with that sort of problem

Well what sort of problem do you deal with? crossed my mind but instead I cooed, "Oh? Could you recommend someone or an agency that perhaps would help me?"

"Hmmmmm? Let me think. I can think of two places you could call; the zoo and the county park rangers."

"I see. How about the city police?"

"I think not in this case."

"I appreciate your help." I said as I hung up the phone.

. . . .

"Cincinnati Zoo," said the male voice over the phone.

"Hello. It was suggested that I call you about this skunk problem I have. It's living under our front porch and I was wondering whether the zoo could assist us in getting rid of it? Maybe trapping it or driving it away from it's burrow?"

"I'm sorry, Sir , but the zoo doesn't get involved with that sort of thing," he said. My, my that sounds familiar. "But," he continued, "I do know of a young girl who is a part time volunteer here at the zoo and she is really into small animals and their habits. Her backyard looks like a miniature zoo. I'll bet she could give you some information on how to get rid of your skunk." Now it's my skunk? "Why don't you give me your name and phone number and I'll ask her to call you?"

"That would be wonderful. Any help at all would be appreciated."

* * *

"My name is Anna Palmero, Mr. Simmer."

"Anna Palmero?" I questioned.

"Yes. Mr. Harper at the zoo . . . ."

"Oh, yes. You're the young lady that has a miniature zoo in her backyard," I cut in.

"I don't know if it's a zoo, but I do have some animals in my backyard," she said with pride in her voice.

"Mr. Harper felt sure that you could help me so here's the problem: I have a skunk living under my front porch and I want to get rid of it. How do I do that?"

"Do you want to kill it?"

"I'd rather not. As much as it is annoying us, I'd rather use that as a last resort."

"Well here are some things you could try. Skunks don't like light so you could put a flashlight or one of those drop lamps they use on cars in the hole. They don't like noise, so maybe a transistor radio would drive it away. They do like peanut butter. Some of that in a trap could help catch it. And let's see . . . oh yeah, they don't like the smell of mothballs. Some of those in the burrow could make it leave."

"All of those things would be helpful except for one thing; they all require getting close to and even into the hole. And none of us relish that task," I said, "but you have been extremely helpful and I thank you for calling. In fact, you have been more help than all the others I called put together. Thanks again."

"You're welcome. I'll call back if I think of anything else," she offered.

Three phone calls and all that's turned up is some peanut butter and mothballs. No physical aid forthcoming from anyone, not even the professionals. "Well, shoot," I thought to myself, "where do I go from here?"

*   *   *

Over the next few days as we continued to feel like prisoners in our own home, skittish that we would bump into the unwelcome guest, I made two more phone calls.

The first went to the park rangers.

"No we don't supply a service to trap animals. But if you don't want to kill it you can get a Hav-A-Heart trap," suggested the ranger.

"What's that.?"

"That's a trap when properly baited will cage the animal without harming it. The cage and animal can be carted off to a likely spot and released. Say like a woods."

"Just how do you get close to a cage with a skunk in it?" I asked.

"Very, very carefully," cracked the ranger.

Doesn't sound like a job for me, the "Great White Hunter."

I thought the second phone call was a stroke of genius on my part. Why didn't I think of this before? Certainly the Environmental Protection Agency would help?

Wrong!!

"You won't help to trap this skunk or get rid of it?" I marveled. "Then what's all this baloney I hear about the EPA and how they're cleaning up our environment and protecting all these helpless wildlife?"

"Sir, the EPA only gets involved with wildlife that is on the endangered species list and a skunk is not on the endangered species list," she lectured.

Well the skunk under my porch should definitely be placed on that list, I thought, as I said, "Sorry to have bothered you.."

"That's perfectly all right. Call anytime."

After this phone call, we continued to fret and curse our plight. Like all good citizens we complained about all these government agencies we've contacted—local, state and federal—and not one has offered a whit of assistance, just lame justifications. When you need some help you can't find those bureaucrats, unless it's election day. Just what are we paying taxes for anyway? And on and on.

" This is the way I would sit at my corner outside, now......

.....I have to sit here looking out the window. Hope that stranger goes away soon."

I wonder why I'm not allowed out after dark anymore? Does it have something to do with that stranger? If it does, I wish they'd let me out 'cause I would keep a sharp eye out for it and not let it sneak up on me like that last time.

And through it all, Kelly, hug her face, was so patient. I don't know if she missed sitting by her corner in the evenings, because she would come in just prior to dusk as soon as we called her. Several times when she didn't show up on schedule we'd race around outside until we found her, engrossed by something that enthralls pussycats. She began to use the top of the living room sofa as one of her favorite resting places. I believe it was because she could keep an eye on her corner from there. She would hop onto the top of the sofa back, take her feline resting pose and, with eyes squinting, keep a check on things.

It was about four o'clock one afternoon. Things were sort of slow at work and my mind drifted to the skunk and all we had done to try to get help. The more I thought about being rejected no matter where we turned, the more frustrated I became. Determined to get some action out of at least one of these agencies, I impulsively picked up the phone and dialed my U.S. Congressman from the First District of Ohio.

"Good afternoon," said an unsuspecting, cheerful voice. "Congressman Gradison's office. How may I help you?"

Reminding myself not to be too gruff with this young lady since she had nothing to do with our present predicament, but wanting to stress the importance of the call, I mustered my best authoritarian voice and said, " I hope you can. No one else seems to be able to. I have this skunk living under my porch and have called every blessed agency I can think of and not one, not one has lifted a finger to help."

"A skunk? One moment ,sir."

Before she put me on hold, I caught the slightest sound of tittering on the other end of the phone. I began smiling at the humor of it all, and realized during the few moments I was on hold she must be telling the whole office about the kook on the phone complaining about a skunk under his porch. Like congressmen have nothing better to do.

"May I help you, sir?" asked a different female voice who was failing at her attempt to conceal her merriment. She must be the kookster; the one who takes care of all important problems.

"I hope you can! I have this skunk living under my porch and I've called the park Rangers, the EPA, the city health commissioner and I don't know who else to call and if I don't get some assistance from the congressman's office my next call is going to President Ford," I said, barely able to hold back my laughter.

"Maybe you should call Carter, too. He may get elected," the voice replied, whereupon neither of us could contain ourselves and we both broke up in laughter.

After order was restored, I asked through several more chuckles, "This must be the weird phone call of the week for you, isn't it?"

"Yes, sir, we do get some odd calls, but let's see if we can help you, okay? What city do you live in? Springdale? Have you called the Springdale police?"

"No, I haven't because I was told they wouldn't help me."

"Who told you that?"

"I believe it was the city Health Commissioner, but I'm not sure because I've talked to so many people they're starting to become hazy."

"All right, sir, let me have your phone number and someone will be getting in touch with you."

"Who'll that be?"

"Probably someone from the Springdale police department. They're usually very helpful in these cases and I'm going to call them and ask why they aren't helping you."

"That will be great," I said as hope of ridding ourselves of that pest rekindled itself.

After I hung up I realized I had given them our home phone number and called Irene to let her know that she may get a call about the skunk and I would explain when I got home. I leaned back in my chair feeling very smug about getting some action from the congressman's office.

My home was about twenty minutes from my place of work. I left work at the usual time and turned the final corner to our house at about five-thirty—a total elapsed time of fifty minutes from the time I had made the phone call to the congressman's office.

SHAZAM! Did I get action.

Three police cars with emergency lights flashing were positioned in front of the house. Two police officers were stationed near the hole with pump shotguns held at the ready on their hips, both closely observing the hose which was flooding water into the hole. Up and down the street there were curb-to-curb kids taking in the action. I looked around for the food and drink vendors but none were around—yet. Neighbors' phones were ringing—as we found out later—with the callers asking, "What's happening at the Simmer's?" Disappointed at the reply, "Oh, it's only a skunk under the porch."

I eased the car to the curb since the police cars had the driveway blocked. Besides I didn't want to get too close for fear of startling the two officers with the shotguns. I made my way out of the car, slowly walked to the house and said to the police with a slight hint of a wave, "Hi. I live here." Meeting no resistance I went inside, located Irene and said, "What in blue blazes is going on out there?"

"Right after you called—I barely hung up the phone when it rang again—I got this call from some lady at the Springdale police. Before I could say hello she said indignantly, "Who said the Springdale police won't help you get rid of a skunk?" And before I knew what was happening those three police cars came roaring up the hill and screeched to a stop in front of the house."

"I never saw anything like it! And that water. I bet it's flooding the basement", I said as I bounded down the basement steps. While inspecting the walls and floor for any signs of water I heard this dull "Krumppff" sound. "Krumppff!" There it goes again. It sounded like a mortar being fired. Running upstairs, I found Irene looking out the front window.

" What's that noise?"

"They gave up on the water and decided to try tear gas. They've fired at least two pellets into the hole," answered Irene.

I looked out the window and saw wisps of smoke coming from the hole. "That burrow must really be long and deep if all that water and tear gas doesn't drive it out of there. Or else . . . ."

Valerie came rushing in and reported, "A funny smell is coming from the basement."

"Great," Irene fumed. It's the tear gas seeping in."

"— that thing isn't even in the hole!"

What's that smell? Don't tell me that stranger is back squirting everything again. My eyes are starting to sting and it is bringing back painful memories. I'm going upstairs and hide 'cause all this noise and confusion and those bright flashing lights have stressed me out. I need some peace and quiet."

"Look, two of the officers are leaving. I wonder what's up?" Mike wondered.

Fifteen minutes later we found out when one of them came to the door and explained, "It looks like we're not going to drive that skunk out of there. So . . . we're going to set up this Hav-A—Heart trap near its burrow and hopefully we can snare it. I'll just go over and help my partner set up the trap."

As they left, the officers reminded us to call if anything got caught or if there was anything else we needed. The curb-to-curb kids disappeared along with the police cars. The neighbors' phones stopped ringing. All we were left with was a twinge of tear gas, a trap, and a skunk. At least they will take care of anything that gets caught. I'll have to call the zoo girl and let her know that water and tear gas are NOT two things that skunks don't like.

That cage looks like my cage except it is made of wire. Wonder what it's for? Every evening Tom or Mommy puts peanut butter into it. I like peanut butter but when they put it in, I'm put in the house so I never get a chance to snatch it. Then every morning Mommy and me go out and inspect the cage, and every morning the peanut butter is gone. I'm confused and still wondering why I'm not let out at night anymore? Must have something to do with that stranger. Only thing I can think of.

For the next ten days we became trap watchers. Each evening one of us would dutifully bait the cage with peanut butter. Irene was usually the first one up in the morning and one of her first chores was to cautiously open the front door a crack and peek out with one eye to view the cage. After the disappointment of not seeing anything in the cage, much less a skunk, she and Kelly would walk over to inspect it more closely and discover that once again the peanut butter was missing. How in the world was that peanut butter being stolen and not trapping the thief?

That stranger must be one clever thief. Or maybe it's some other bandit. All I know is a lot of peanut butter is being used and I'm not getting any of it.

The mystery was solved quite by accident one evening. After placing a fresh glob of peanut butter in the cage, Irene and I retired to the rear of the house for some well earned loafing. While enjoying our break, Irene spied this cat—whom we called "Big Orange" not knowing it's real name—sneaking across our side lawn in the general direction of the cage.

On a hunch, Irene quietly got up, slipped to the front of the house, and from a concealed position affording a good view of the cage, waited and watched. Sure enough! Here comes Big Orange creeping toward the cage, stopping now and then with one paw suspended in mid-air to take a cautious look around him. He reaches the cage, sniffs around ever so cautiously, then gingerly thrusts his paw and leg into the cage, spears the peanut butter with his claws, withdraws his loot and daintily enjoys his daily treat. And then, always the cat, cleans his paws and face after enjoying his prize.

No wonder we can't nab that skunk.

* * *

A few days later the cage was taken away by the police as they had told us they would do, since it was needed elsewhere. In two weeks it had caught a few blades of grass, leaves and some peanut butter smears. I guess it will be put in place so it can provide another cat or bandit with peanut butter treats.

Irene and I discussed our plight and decided the only way we were ever going to get rid of that skunk was to do it ourselves.

The first thing we tried was blocking the hole with a large fieldstone (Our development was known as "Rock City") since they were in plentiful supply, thinking if the hole was blocked the skunk would find another home.

Naturally the chore fell to me to get close to the hole. During the day, a quick dash to the hole, a plop, and a quicker retreat got me to a safe distance. The next morning an inspection of the area revealed another hole had appeared right next to the boulder! All the skunk had done was to make a slight detour. Outsmarted again by a wild thing. "Nature" was fast becoming a four letter word for us. I made another dash to and from the hole to discard the worthless fieldstone.

That evening we went shopping for mothballs.

The problem was who was going to get close enough to put them in the hole? None of us relished the task even in the daytime, as my dashes to and from the hole with the fieldstone testified to.

"Okay, here's the plan. We can't be sure when that thing leaves its burrow in the evening, so we will each take turns looking out from the front window to watch for it. When it leaves I'll get out on the front porch roof—you can look down the hole from there—and drop these mothballs into the hole," I instructed. Snickering from my co-conspirators? "What's so funny," I said defensively.

"Why can't you just put the mothballs in the hole, Dad," Mike smirked.

"Yeah, why not?", grinned Irene. "Why do you have to get up on the roof to do it?"

I gazed at my tormentors knowing full well that they knew why I was dropping those mothballs, rather than putting them into the hole.

"Here's the problem. I don't want to get too close to that hole even during the day. I know, I know," I said waving my arms before they could butt in, "it's not supposed to come out in the day. But, suppose we do see the skunk leave and all of a sudden it changes its mind and comes back and finds one of us leaning over the hole? Do you want to be that one? Well? Any volunteers? No? Then it's up on the roof and it'll be 'moth balls away'."

Sure have a lot of company this evening on my sofa. Like me, they're looking over the top of the sofa. Just kneeling over the top and watching. Maybe they're looking for the stranger, too. I saw it a couple of times the last few days walking across the porch, but no one was around that I could tell. I just watched as it walked across the street and to the other house. Here comes Valerie. It must be her turn.

The kids were in their rooms doing homework when Irene was on watch. Suddenly the thing appeared. She sounded the alarm with a hushed but piercing, "It's coming out." The kids bounded down the stairs and the three of us made a mad dash to the sofa.

Hey. They're all here. Now maybe they'll see what I've been watching all these evenings.

"Where is it? Where is it? I whispered?" Why everybody was speaking so quietly I don't know. We probably could have turned on a siren and that thing wouldn't have cared less it was that brazen.

"There! Right by the front tree," Irene murmured. "Look, it's going toward the street."

"Well, I could have told you that if you had asked. It does this every night but none of you are ever around when I'm sitting on top of the sofa so I couldn't tell you. Sometimes it even looked up at me as if to say, " You want more of this, cat!?" All I could do was stare back.

We watched the creature as it wobbled its way to the curb, crossed the street, scaled the opposite curb, now stopping to warily look about its surroundings, then continued across Keene's front yard finally disappearing behind Keene's house.

"I wonder where it's going?" Valerie questioned.

"I don't know but I hope it stays there!" Irene said adamantly. "Before you got to the window, that bold thing came out of it's hole, got up on the porch, walked along the porch under the window—right under my nose—to the front step, stepped off the porch and crossed the lawn to the tree where you first saw it. What nerve! I'll bet it would have done that even if I had been on the porch!"

"Now you see why I don't want to get near it, because it does seem to be pretty fresh. Well it's time for me to get on the roof. Someone keep watch and let me know if they spot it coming back."

Kelly followed me upstairs sensing something big was happening. I went into our master bedroom and climbed out through a window to the roof. Kelly tried to jump out too and I had to shoo her back in.

Come on, Tom. I want to see what's happening. Oh. Okay, I'll wait here.

On the roof I could see a "bomber's moon" was out. Good, I thought, I'll have no problem seeing the hole. I positioned myself over the roof edge and one by one started dropping mothballs down toward the hole. Missed! Missed again! Now I dropped a few at a time. No good. The wind was blowing them off course. I stop to scan the area to see if it's coming back. No sign of it and nothing from the lookouts down below. I drop more handfuls. OK! Some of them are getting into the hole. What the heck , I think, might as well dump a box at a time. I tilt the box over the hole and carpet-bomb around the hole. Some have landed on the porch and in nearby shrubs and trees. A couple of crazy ones are nestled on the front windowsill. The contents of three more boxes go the route of the first box. Mothballs seem to be everywhere. It looks as if it snowed in one section of our yard. I think, if skunks don't like the smell of mothballs there shouldn't be one of them within three blocks of our house, as I climbed back through the window.

Tom? Tom? What happened out there? What are all those little snowballs doing all over our yard? Tom's running down the stairs so fast I can't keep up with him. Guess I'm not going to get any answers. I'll just have to inspect the area tomorrow.

Before I left for work the next morning, we approached the hole. Mothballs were still scattered everywhere. It was difficult to tell whether or not anything had disturbed them during the night. We inspected very closely. No clues. Was the skunk gone?

These snowballs have a funny smell to them. In a way they smell pretty good, but I wouldn't want to get caught in a small space with them.

*   *   *

Irene was waiting on the front porch when I arrived home from work. As I got out of the car she said, "Come see what I've done," and led me to the hole. "See, I've swept the mothballs into the hole and left some just around the entrance." The place certainly looked different. The mothballs were out of the bushes, off the windowsills and porch, and the lawn looked green again.

"I just got so crazy today about that thing and how we seemed to be its prisoners that I grabbed a broom, marched out there, swept the mothballs where they were supposed to be, smoothed the ground around the entrance, all the time daring that thing to come out; I was going to swat it with the broom handle if it did!"

"Weren't you scared."

"Of course, but I was determined it wasn't going to run my life anymore!" Irene said with a glint in her eyes. I've seen that glint before and had learned not to mess with it.

"Honey, I'm proud of you, but why did you smooth the dirt around the entrance?"

" I thought we could see footprints better that way. Then we'll know for sure if it's still going in and out of the hole."

" Great idea," I said.

A few days went by without anyone noticing any activity in or around the hole. Before, one of us would spot it around the house, but now . . . . . . nothing. Our hopes were at a high. Did we finally get rid of it? Were the mothballs the stake in the heart? A few more days passed without seeing any sign of the skunk. But, there was always that uncertainty however small. Irene solved the problem with another one of her ideas. She simply spread flour in and around the hole!

A week went by with no signs of footprints on the flour even though the flour was freshened and inspected each day. Our next move was to shovel pebbles (Rock City strikes again) and dirt into the hole, pack it down and cover the whole affair with the previously discarded fieldstone. No detour tunnels appeared.

It—must—be—gone!

Hey, this is great. All of a sudden I'm allowed out again at night. I missed my corner and guarding my porch. Wonderful to be out again in the evening enjoying the view and the quiet. All my humans seemed to be delirious about something. They were whooping and hollering—what carrying on. But, I'll tell you something; I'm still looking over my shoulder in case that stranger decides to come back. If it does I'll scratch its eyes out before it can squirt me again. Ahhh. Nice, out here.

A number of years have passed since the skunk episode. The faint odor of tear gas has long since dissipated, Kelly stopped smelling like a skunk when she cleaned herself, she reigns supreme in her domain once again, and we can enjoy our evenings on the porch. Life returned to normal. We will forever be grateful to a young girl whose knowledge of small animals led us to the method of eviction that was kindest to all parties.

*   *   *

A few months after the skunk had left, Irene and I were relaxing in lawn chairs by the pool when Valerie appeared and asked, "Mom. Dad. Did you hear about the Brent's dog?"

"No," we replied, "what happened?"

"It got squirted by a skunk last night!"

"Oh, no," said Irene, shaking her head in disbelief. "I think we just found out where our skunk landed."

"Yeah," I said nonchalantly, "maybe you should call the Brents and tell them all about mothballs."

VI

And So Goodbye

Here comes the carrier again. I really, really don't want to get into that thing today. I just don't feel right. But I'll have to purr and bear it.

That car ride seemed to last forever, but I'm glad that's over. I'm feeling worse but the guy with the glass thingy said, "It's OK." He should feel like me. Can't wait to get home. At least on the way home I don't ride in the carrier. Can't seem to get comfortable. I'll get up with Mommy. Are we there yet? At last. The fresh air is wonderful. I feel unsteady on my feet. Oops! I almost fell over. What's wrong with me? I need a drink of water. Mommy, I don't feel good. I can hardly walk. The water dish seems so far away. Think I'll lie down. Can't get my breath. Mommy is on the phone. Still can't reach the water, Now we're rushing back to the car. No carrier. Oh, Mommy, Mommy help me. I can't breathe. I ca . . . .

*   *   *

Kelly was with us for about fourteen years. But, one evening on returning home from an out-of-town business trip, Irene was waiting for me on the front porch wiping the tears from her eyes. Getting out of the car I heard the terrible news that Kelly had passed on. We hugged each other and cried like babies. The Vet said she had had a massive stroke and that she had not suffered. Her ashes were scattered around her favorite resting place. Her corner.

Kelly was a joy to us and we loved her to pieces.. She always gave us kussas and looked for a lap to leap into to take her daily siestas while working on her 23 hours of daily sleep. And of course we always thought she was the cat's meow, but we never realized how special she was until one day when Irene had her at the Vet's for her usual checkup.

While other visitor's were busy cringing and cowering with tail between their legs, our Kelly was serenely snoozing on Irene's lap while waiting her turn. A lady who was also waiting smiled at Irene and said, "My that's a pretty cat. Is she a special breed.?" Irene, bursting with pride and barely able to contain herself, gave Kelly a gentle hug and replied, "Only to us. Only to us."

After all these years we still talk to her photo.

Memories

" Happy B'day, Mike."

"Me, Valerie, Mike, Tom and Irene. Hope I get a drumstick."

" I love you, mommy."

" Love you, Tom."

" Even Gabby likes to walk with Tom and me."

" Let's go to the park."

" Now they've dressed me like a dog."

" Gee? What happened to the grass?"